Split

poems by

Joanne Matone Samraney

Finishing Line Press
Georgetown, Kentucky

Split

*In loving memory of
my parents, Daniel & Julia Matone
& my sister, Diana Kotcho*

Publisher: Leah Maines

Editor: Christen Kincaid

Cover Art and Design: Jamie Benjamin

Author Photo: Marlo Samraney Oswald

.

Printed in the USA on acid-free paper.
Order online: www.finishinglinepress.com
        also available on amazon.com

Author inquiries and mail orders:
Finishing Line Press
P. O. Box 1626
Georgetown, Kentucky 40324
U. S. A.

Table of Contents

PRAYER

God, grant me
no accolades
Swiss bank accounts
mansions or Jaguars.
Silence the rant in my heart
with the pulse of my breathing
to Beethoven's Moonlight Sonata
my little book of poems
the scent of eucalyptus
rising from the light
of a single candle

One

How many caskets must we enter
before we disappear

-JMS

Moon's Child

My swollen body floats
In this shallow pond.
Fish with teeth
sharp as my father's
nibble at my feet.
My feet belong to the fish
living under the moon.
It is the moon who mirrors
the face of my mother.
She sits on a rock. She laments.
"We must be like fish.
We must swim upstream."
Her tired arm tugs at the black net
twisted between my thighs
until threads break and water
pulls the graceful body
of my daughter away from me.
Upstream she swims,
her young breasts float
like soft white lilies.
Her small pink mouth
opens and closes
like the mouth of a fish.

Red Hen

Cousin Gabe asks, "Why are we eating raw chicken?" I don't have an answer for him.

Anything can happen in a dream.

We come into the world raw because we are meant to be transparent,
before the world decides to dress us then say,
shame, shame see what you've become.

Or, maybe we are cannibals, intent on poisoning ourselves.

My neighbors, Josephine and Glen want to eat raw chicken with us.
Josephine is afraid to die, but dies anyway. Glen is still alive.

And now it seems the red hen paddling frantically above water is me.

When death comes for me, I don't want to be a chicken. I want to be raw.

There Is a Thief Who Robs From Us

Autumn arrives uninvited.
She fills your life
with too many dead leaves.
My arms have grown weary
trying to rake them
from your roots.

There is so much
left to share, to say
before snow falls over us.

I want to spend a whole afternoon
talking with you.
I want to know
what you dreamed as a child.
Did you hate that woman
who fed you dry bread in a dark room
after you ironed her husband's white shirts?
Was Sister JoAnne the first to tell you
how beautiful you really were?
Is that why you named me JoAnne?

Mother, I want to touch your wrinkled hands
and tell you how happy I am
that my hands have stopped washing dishes
and started writing poetry.

I want to tell you
I think there is a woman you hide;
a woman who is not
as important to you
as your husband and children,
a woman inside that never grew old;
would still leave
her mother-in-law's party to go to the theater;
a woman you try to abort.

Mrs. Angelo's Daughter

The aunts don't seem to mind me here beside them
playing with my paper dolls. They say
my ears are big, but my head is small.

They say Mrs. Angelo will bake cookies
for my Holy Communion
but Mrs. Angelo scares me. She hurt Katie.
They say Katie went to the hospital
to get sewed back up.

They say Katie wears too much make-up,
stays out all night, drinks too much.
Drink, drink! I shout at my paper dolls.
No one hears me.

I tell my paper dolls,
Hurry, clean up the blood.
I hate that old coat hanger.
It made Katie cry,
turned Katie's legs red
like her pretty long hair.
I name my red-hair doll, Katie.

I don't want Mrs. Angelo
to bake my Holy Communion cookies.

On The Eve of Christmas

I kneel in a dim foyer
in a row house on Wayne Street.

The infant lies in a manger
under a tree bubbling with color.

One frayed stocking hangs empty
on a mantel near a cracked window.

Through the silence of glass
my cold hand warms to my father,

hand swollen purple and red around his shovel's
persistent push of coal down our cellar chute.

Your Path

You tell me
you walk straight;
ahead of me
behind your father.
If you fall
I catch you.
If you veer left or right
I center you.
If I walk
next to you
you cannot focus.
Ahead
your father holds onto
the leash around your neck
pulling hard.

You say
this leash grows
longer when you disagree.
I say be kind
my son.
Soon your father's eyes
will deceive him
and you
will run ahead
while I walk
behind with him.
For now,
your father needs
something to hold onto.

Chicken Soup

Her silence throbs like my tongue
scorched from milk, too hot;

but I begin to imagine the comfort
of her breasts against my cheek.

In the kitchen
the plucked chicken floats in a pot of hot water.

On the porcelain stove
bubbles dance around cubes of celery and onions.

Once this past week, I thought I heard her call
but the voice dissipated like hot steam on cold windows.

Leaving only a stream
streaking down my cheeks.

It will take years to soothe this scorch
of hot milk from my tongue.

I Wished You Rose

You insisted peony, like you,
a pale pink drained of blood.

If I could I would
cut you from the dead
place you in a vase
feed you fresh water
keep your color pink
your petals soft.

Yet I understand
the nature of peonies,
how they allow ants to stick
even after they open;
how they allow ants
to bury themselves
deep inside.
.
But death brings its own
insistence   silence
on this first Mother's Day
without you
as I plant on your grave
a rose, thick with thorns,
to chase ants away.

Roots

I will never eat sweet potatoes
without tasting that afternoon
Dad asked me to stay awhile,
eat some dinner with him.

He sat in Mum's chair.
His jacket hung alone on his.
What's new? he asked
as he unfolded yesterday's news.

Go ahead, he insisted.
Eat a sweet potato with me.
They're good for you.
Can't I said, *have to get*
home to the kids.

How could I know
cleaning their house,
preparing his dinner
could not fill that empty chair.

How could I know
I would return to their kitchen
each time I smell
a sweet potato baking

sit with him awhile longer
try to erase shadows
on their kitchen window,
coax the light back in.

Anxiety, My Familiar

Back again pulling
at my neck, chewing
through my stomach,
squeezing my mouth dry.
How tired you must be
after years of wrapping
your long arms around my heart,
pulling, pulling.

Wretched old man, you do not
understand the planting and transplanting
of my father's chestnut tree,
those twisted roots in worn arms
dragged from his home to mine.
Such tenderness, my hands binding
burlap over loosened dirt
shoveling more inside--
yet another open hole.

Pity this exhausted tree
unable to yield fruit.
Pity this little girl
growing old, reaching
beyond fallen leaves.

Returning

Before you leave I want to tell you how
it feels to dip a tiny sponge in water
and watch your tongue search for Mother's breast.
Before you leave I want to tell you how
it feels to close my eyes as you lie naked
in pain. Once you covered your eyes while I
labored to birth the grandson named for you.
And now with you I breathe to machines ticking
your life away. You put your hand in mine
and say, *I want to go home.* But, before
you leave me, please tell me how your
daughter can become her Father's mother.

What You Must Never Forget

You must never forget your first trolley ride,
how you sat in the back next to your mother
convinced the bearded man in front
reading a newspaper and picking his teeth
was out to get you, would take you away.
That was the first time you sensed danger
although you were too young to name it.
You sensed it the way a baby wren senses
when he is about to be captured, the way
you sensed it that day in the grocery store
when you began sorting the multicolored coupons
while you waited for your mother at the checkout counter
until your hand slipped and a rainbow
of colors scattered at your feet.
It was danger that made you run
out of the store without your mother,
run as fast as you could home
to your father sitting barefoot on your porch swing,
string in hand, ready to pull
the upright shoe box over a baby wren.

When You Told Me You Had Leukemia

If you should die before me,
ask if you could bring a friend.
            Stone Temple Pilots

It was a cool October evening.
The two of us together at last,

sipping wine and catching up
on the ordinary tales of our lives.

We heard the crow's caw outside,
saw a flash of black wings,

the color of a nun's habit,
the color of fear   of death.

Still, we talked of our grandchildren,
laughed at our own childhood,

how in first grade I erased my arithmetic paper,
gave it to you when you forgot yours,

how you took it without hesitation,
wrote your name over mine.

That's how it was   still is,
one of us first the other blending in.

You had a boyfriend first,
introduced me to his friend.

We both wore pink at our senior prom.
Our dates wore black.

Two Walnuts on My Desk

An office Christmas party, I, the only employee
who received two walnuts from the Big Boss.
The message was clear. My struggle was over.
I put them on my desk, two walnuts from the Big Boss.

His male Assistant was envious. His male Comptroller
was envious. I, his HR Director in a red dress and red lipstick
had two walnuts on my desk.

One day the Foreman on the road crew came
into my office, saw two walnuts on my desk
and cracked one with his little finger.

Still I, the HR Director in a red dress and red lipstick
kept two walnuts from the Big Boss on my desk,
one cracked, one intact.

And the Foreman, well the Foreman sustained
a busted bone in his pinky.

I Can Only Imagine

what the room looks like, that bright light
blinding your brown eyes, the green walls,
the figures dressed in green shirts and pants,
the white masks covering their mouths.

You lying on a long black padded table,
a white sheet hiding the quiver of your small body,
all except for your naked left breast, black as night
and blue as the surgeon's eyes

glaring through the silver scalpel in her hand,
all those many shiny scalpels, hooks, needles, forceps
and the gauze, white and sterile on the table.
No one familiar there to hold your hand, listen

for the bleep of the machine counting
each of your shallow breaths. No one
to assure your breast will still be there
after you close your eyes and

open them to a new morning.

Yellow

When I wheel her into the garden
I leave her door open just a bit,
afraid I might lock us out and she
might become the wild lion
I imagined she was in another life.
I expect whiskers to sprout
from the creases around her mouth,
her gray hair to become
a full yellow mane.

Not this old woman with eyes that seem
to disintegrate before my own,
not this old woman who doesn't
recognize her brothers or sisters
or who I am to her.
She asks for her husband
dead thirty years,
says he is never hungry.

I tell her the garden is filled
with buttercups, ask if she would like
me to pick a few. *They are yellow*
I say. *What is your favorite color?*
Yellow, she says and I want
to dress her in yellow, happy as the sun,
happy as the woman who carried
a wooden table from the basement
to her kitchen for Sunday dinners.

When Love Speaks

She says,
I did not promise you
hands touching silver hair
nor even one more moon
to wrap around your dark dreams.

I have warned you of bees
yet smelled honey
on your breath;
and of spiders who hide
your nakedness under
their spool of magic thread.

Think of how I caught you.
Think of how I freed you.
Think of me hiding my own
nakedness under my spool
of silver threads.

Separate

So you think you ripped
me from your heart
after months of crawling in
then out of my web

I'll be back.
Some morning a tiny bubble
in your coffee
breaking then blending.

In April the hint
of my blush—
July the fire
on your tongue—

October,
in a night full of crickets,
the sound of laughter
in that room,
laughter that drowns out nights
drowns out crickets.

And in December, when
you haven't dreamed of me for weeks
you'll wake to the echo of crystals
splitting on your bedroom window;
tiny crystals splitting
again and again
dropping from heaven and splitting
and splitting.

Even At Five

I felt the shame
of running topless
in the rain.
It was the way
Eddie looked at me.
The way my small
nipples stiffened
when he gave me
his big tooth smile;
the way I ran
to hide in the alley
where I sat alone,
one arm wrapped
around my chest,
the other pulling
at the frayed elastic
on my cotton underwear.

Dreamer

When I asked, you said
you did not love me
would marry someone else.
And you did
in real life. After all
I only meet you in my dreams
even then, you barely speak to me
as if you never knew me.

Forty years is a long time
not to see someone you loved.
The other night, I found you
in some sort of hospital.
(Everyone is in some sort
of hospital these days.)
Your door was shut.

My son went in to visit you.
When I knocked, you came out,
that familiar grin across your mouth.
The room was dark, a cave I think,
cold with dirt walls. It smelled
of feces and marijuana, and why
was my son in there with you?

It's difficult growing old,
marshmallow arms, a belly,
pregnant with desire
for something
anything more awake.

Bedtime Story
for Nina

Strach my back Guggy and tell me a story.
And so the Grandmother leans closer and begins:

Once upon a time there was a little girl...

It doesn't matter what story is told
or how many times the child has heard it.

What matters is the small child
cradled in her grandmother's arms,

The feel of warm fingers
on the child's skin,

the lull of a her Grandmother's
voice in her ear,

The scent of just washed hair
brushing against her Guggy's lips.

After Reading Robert Bly's Morning Poems

You interrupted my sleep again last night.
Made me pose for a photograph with your family.
You had two sisters. I knew you didn't have sisters
but confided in the short one anyway, told her
I worried your wife would be angry.
Two men on motorcycles mocked me in the background.
I knew they would. I thought I killed them
when I pushed them down the grassy slope.
Like you, they didn't die.

October in Pittsburgh

I saw her again
today on Second Avenue,
arms folded around her torn blue jeans
head drooping in her lap,
two strands of brown hair
falling across her young face.
I thought of my granddaughters,
my daughter.

Silence said, *pick her up.*
Ask her name. Take her home.
Feed her lunch, then
brush her hair.

Deafened by the constant rumble
of wheels spiraling in my mind,
I continued driving, past
an occasional young Maple
between sidewalk and street,
their faded red leaves still clinging
before the final shuffle, the silent
crash against an apathetic sidewalk.

Canning Tomatoes

My husband wants me
to can tomatoes with him
and suddenly I am
in that damp basement on Wayne Street.
Mother wears a stained apron.
My sister and I timidly wait

for our signal to begin,
that first slit of skin,
the exposed pulp.
Acid burns our nostrils.
Bell jars boil on a blackened stove.
Their steady clink
threaten summer's end
like this shrill of cicadas
through our screen door.
I turn to my husband
and say, *no.*
I am afraid of not sealing
lids tight enough,
boiled water toppling,
jars shattering, smeared hands
sifting through chunks of tomatoes
not able to put the pieces
back together again.

The Prize

Think of life as a wide river.
Think of yourself
standing alone at its bank.

A silver flash darts across the murk.
How did it happen
here in the shadow of carp?

An illusion?
You watch it disappear
appear.

You want to grab it
hold it, taste it.
Already the ease

of pink flesh
sliding lightly
between your teeth,

the succulence
on your tongue.
You watch and wait.

It appears, disappears
in a barrage of carp surfacing.
You want to dive in after it

but your body stiffens
recognizes the mystery
of going too deep,

the agony of coming back up
covered with muck
a dead salmon in your hand.

The Music Room at Niagara on the Lake

My husband drifts off to sleep.
Tomorrow, forty-three years of marriage.
Tonight, I'll imagine making love
to the music of Rosina Wachtmeister.
Her painting, *Composition for Piano and Cello*
hangs on the wall opposite our bed.
Cello and music sheets ready.
Where is the piano? Where is the musician?

My husband lies snoring on the left side
of our anniversary bed beside Rosina's
other painting of piano, music sheets
and an empty piano bench. Where is the pianist?
A violin hangs on my side of our anniversary bed,
Where is the bow? Where is the music

in this burgundy room of roses—roses
on the door, roses on the violin, roses
on the bed sheets, roses on the quilt
of our anniversary bed. Where is the musician?

Mike the Bum

Most mornings he woke on the side of the dock where The Pittsburgh Press drivers loaded their trucks. He never talked, never begged. Before leaving the dock some drivers would toss him a couple bucks, loose pocket change. On cold days, he slept in the cab of his favorite driver's truck while the driver loaded papers for the day. This driver was the only one who talked to him like he was a real person, asked how he felt, if he was hungry, told him *have a nice day*, and handed him a fin, enough for five beers. The others didn't know he was a former boxer, never noticed his sad but kind, blue eyes, his sandy hair sprinkled with gray, always in need of a shampoo. They didn't know he ate at the *Improvement of the Poor or St. Joseph's House of Hospitality* when he was hungry; didn't know he read torn books from the dumpster when he was sober. Not seeing his favorite driver for a few days, he wondered. No one told him about the accident, Shadyside Hospital, the internal injuries, a broken back. Finally he asked. Without a word, he hitched a ride to the hospital, stopped off at the men's room, combed his hair with his fingers, slapped water on his face, dried it with a paper towel, cleaned his few teeth with his right index finger and antiseptic soap, then tucked his faded maroon shirt with holes and missing buttons into his tattered khaki pants. One last look in the bathroom mirror and off he went to the third floor, room three sixteen. I, the driver's wife, hesitated until he held his hand out and said, *Hi, I'm Mike the Bum. I'm here to see my friend.*

My Green Velvet Purse

The shrinking is gradual
as the expanded wires
lock under the gold clasp
concealing
popsicle pink lipstick
the bluebirds embroidered
on my lace handkerchief
and of course
the rosary beads.
Mother warned
Never go anywhere
without your rosary.
As though cold hard
crystals could bring me comfort.
There is no comfort in crystals
only in the touch of exposed
velvet gathering at the opening
where the whole being
comes together
under that crucial cap of gold.

Birthday Present

For Diana
9/14/1946 – 4/23/2013

When you gave it to me
I didn't want it. I didn't tell you
but thought, *not my taste.*
as I politely mouthed, *thank you.*

Later I slid it, still in its wrapping,
under my dresser thinking *too gaudy*
I'll never wear it. Why ruin a perfectly
solid brown sweater with so many gold sequins

These days I sit by your bedside in a plain white T-shirt
as you lie helpless in your blue cotton hospital gown.
Your sunken chest heaves up and down
in short uneven breaths.

And all I can think of is you,
my little sister squinting in the sun
as we traded under our backyard picnic table
your peach pie for me, my round steak for you.

And all I can think of is you,
my teenage sister dancing at Burke Glen Ballroom,
the smile on your face as you sang,
"This is Dedicated to the One I love."

And all I can think of are your many gifts to me
that were *not my taste* and that gaudy brown
sequined sweater under my dresser
with the glitter that was so much you.

The Arc of Nothingness

I'll find you here, my God
among those lying
in the soil of darkness

those not yet born
those born again,
all creatures split in half—

one eye
watching the other
one foot

ahead of the other
one hand
hidden from the other

here where the double womb
virgins reside
where the graves of the dead

open to the Father
of double heads
here in the arc of nothingness.

Illusion

Who is this woman posing
in my bedroom mirror?
One spotted hand holds
a dust mop, the other, a bucket.

Tell her to wipe that gray
blur covering her eyes
and look at me.

I am not the woman she sees
with sagging knees, arms spread
as though sacrificed on a cross.

I am a young woman in a sleek
black dress that lightly brushes
the tips of satin sandals.
Skin the color of a ripe peach.
Lips parted and full.

Two

To enter the sacred
one must climb the ladder
of her own cave

-JMS

Weed

Early morning, here

and there sprinkles

of violets, buttercups,

a lone dandelion.

Tell me, who decides

what is weed, what is flower.

Split

I don't want to be Carm, my mother's oldest sister
who took care of her brothers and sisters,
didn't finish high school, became an office clerk
and didn't cry when her father died
two weeks before her wedding.

I want to be Angie, my mother's other sister, who danced
the last dance at Kennywood Danceland,
hopped the last train home, while her sisters
prayed the rosary by their old console radio hoping
nothing tragic happened to Angie and she'd
get home before their poppa woke.

I don't want to be Carm who taught me
how to make beds with hospital tucks,
how to wash and fold clothes
and prepare supper for our family
before my mother got home from work.

I want to be Angie who stayed up past midnight on
Christmas Eve to bake thumbprint cookies with
red and green jelly, sew taffeta dresses for our dolls
and climb up Grandma's roof to jingle bells
so we kids would think Santa arrived
and finally drift off to sleep.

I don't want to be Carm who saved her money
only to live her last days in a nursing home
and think her son was her dead husband.

I want to be Angie who left dishes in the sink overnight,
played jacks with her great nieces on her kitchen floor in winter,
picked violets with them in spring.

Julia

I clutch the wringer washer
in our cellar on Wayne Street.
Unable to stop the rusty agitator,
it thrusts my blue sun dress
from side to side while you fill
both laundry tubs with cold water.

Be careful of your fingers
you warn, as I untangle
my dress from the machine
and squeeze it
between two wooden rollers.
It drops down into the first rinse.

Much like your hand slumps back
into the wave of your blue negligee
this afternoon as I bend over you
remove the red ruby from your cold finger,
kiss your closed eyes
green like the ocean
and miles away.

To Find Your Soul

look in the dark
eyes of your dog.
Stroke her body
until black hair shimmers
blue through fingertips.

Dip a bare brush
in a rainbow of paints
poured in small jars
along the ledge
of the artist's easel;

Core the layers of your heart
as if it were a plump red apple
spilling seeds in a labyrinth of purple poppies,
delicate details of exposed
stamen and petal.

Only in release of the hidden
can one find the golden thread
that links all living things
to a god buried deep in dark waters.

Black Cat

No one loves you.
They say you're an omen.
I say you're sleek as midnight,
a stranger knocking on my door.
Your eyes, a promise of emeralds,
an escape from my grandmother's small bathroom

where I peek through a cracked door
at my uncle bathing in her claw tub
where I imagine being chased
by a grizzly bear and flushed
down the cesspool of lust
with other drowned animals.

Anything can happen in the dark.

I am the buxom blond
Can Can dancer on my shower curtain.
My eyes are lined in black.
My lips are painted red.
The little guy in my hand is as naked as his desire.
I am ready

to make a meal of him.
There is one feather left on that proud rooster.
I'll pluck it out then toast his flabby flesh until it sizzles.

Anything can happen in the dark.

I Want To Be One of Those Green Beans in the Photograph On The Fifth Floor of Shadyside Hospital

I am tired of running a marathon
with the digital clock
in my bedroom, tired
of brushing my teeth and flushing
someone else's waste down the commode,
tired of smiling at irate customers
and reading business letters with too many words,
tired of covering too many wrinkles
with too much make-up and catching my new
pantyhose on an open desk drawer.

Tired of watching people I love grow old and
weak shriveling in their thin worn skin.

I want to be one of those green beans
in the photograph on the fifth floor
of Shadyside Hospital;
tossed from some old farmer's stained apron
to the wind, fresh and fat
exposing my bulges, free and unashamed
strings dangling from my long body
like unattached umbilical cords
too high to be reached, too high
to be picked and snipped
and shoved in a can
left to drown in pickling juice
soggy and limp as the rest.

The Music of Boxes

Around me boxes fall
one over the other;
inside
a yellowed satin gown
a rusty harmonica
letters brittle now
as the hands that wrote them.
I shake them.
I kick them.
I hug them.
I kiss them.
I kneel in homage
to these treasures;
to my parents
who left me
with arms that wrap
one over the other;
hands that open
one over the other;
and knees that rock
to the music of boxes.

Grounded Angels

Uncle Pellegrino hides in the corner
covering another Rolling Rock.
The sisters are disgusted. I see it on their faces.
Things haven't changed much here.

Uncle Aqualino argues with the stranger in dark glasses
over President Bush's Energy Plan as if
that matters where they're going.

They've been standing here
for over thirty years.
Grandma seems taller than the rest.
Aunt Angie must have stuffed
paper in her shoes like she did
for Cousin Mark when he wanted
to ride the roller coasters in Kennywood.

It's cold standing under their shadows.
My mother offers to button my worn overcoat,
but I can't reach her extended hand.

I recognize the music made by the man
with two missing fingers and a golden saxophone.
He has been standing here the longest
and still Grandma has not called to him,
Mio figlio, venire qui.

I could swear Aunt Lucia just tapped my shoulder.
When I turn around, I see a single
yellow butterfly floating above my head.

All aboard the conductor calls
as Grandma lowers her baby, Alfredo,
from her arms onto the platform,
then unknots the white handkerchief
pulled from the faded blue
smock covering her breasts.

"*Uno, due, tre, quattro,*
cinque, sei, sette, otto."
She still has two coins left.
She motions to the conductor to go on without them.
She will wait for her other two children,
The two standing with me across the tracks.

Beyond

She's in this photograph
by Alfred Stieglitz
somewhere
behind Mount Williamson.
I walk past the rocks
follow the glimmer of sun
trickling through the cleavage
of two large mounds.
I'll find her there, obvious
as she was in my dream last night
when two nuns with leaden crosses
led me past a chain of gothic altars
and waiters with white towels
folded in the crease of their arms,
showed me to a table for two in the corner.
There, a younger version of my mother
greets me. Her hair black,
her eyes green with kindness.
You're still alive I whisper.
Not everyone can see me
she says and takes my hand.
We walk behind an alcove
that shelters a woman in a concrete casket.
She wears a blue space suit and looks
like a wax figure of my mother,
only darker. *Do the dead live*
on another planet?
Her silence, larger than
the mist shadowing the sun
in Stieglitz's photograph,
larger than what hides beyond
the door that will not open.

Grandfather

I

The bald man with a silver mustache
 lifts me onto a white porcelain cabinet.

I smell tomatoes
and earth under his fingernails.

Quanto Vecchio Tu? he asks in Italian.
Due I say holding up two fingers.

He places two dollars between them, hangs
his sweater on the brass hook above my head.

II

Grandma said he was sleeping the day she wrapped her hand
around mine, walked me to the silver box in their parlor.

I seldom ventured below the second level of his cellar
knowing this is where he made wine

remembering large black hoses
along the galley in the concrete floor

wooden barrels scattered on the side.
The sour smell of fermented wine.

The Storyteller

For Michie

My husband likes to sip whiskey
in strong black coffee and tell stories
to little children, says
he doesn't sugar-coat them.
His hundred-year-old grandmother was a witch.
His sister, Loretta, poisoned her by giving her
iced tea without sweetener,
but we know he exaggerates.

He doesn't understand real truth,
the grandmother leaning over a hot stove
warming hands that lived too long,
dug too many days through thick black earth,
grew peaches, corn, coffee beans,
prized long-stem roses to lay the first day in May
at her Blessed Mother's chipped ceramic feet.

Love Song

The window of the white frame
house on James Street
opens wide.
I am nine years old, and
Grandma lives there;
a tiny woman, wearing a
white cooking cap.
She stands stirring
red sauce that will multiply
like the five barley loaves and two fish.

Outside,

the boys play ball
waiting for the fruit
on her peach trees
to ripen.
All day, I wait
for Tony Gooda's green truck.
It creaks down the street
like Grandma's swing.
Even the chickens wake.
Mrs. Bosco, Mrs. Bosco, Io ho
delle belle pesche mature oggi.

In the evening
her cracked hands
peel the peaches' rough skin.
Their taste is as sweet as
the young girl in Italy
listening to a poor
young farmer sing as
he tills her father's land.

At night
I lie in the soft
feathers of their bed.

I can smell the sweat
from that farmer.
The sound of the train
whistle mutes.
I can hear her singing
that same song.

Your Green Plaid Shirt

Tonight I want to remember your green plaid shirt;
the way my skin melted in the soft flannel
and my tired arms relaxed in the long loose sleeves.
I want to remember how your smile
made me blush.
You said I looked cute. You said
I made you smile.
I could make you do anything then.
Tonight I want to remember how your gentle fingers
unfastened the brown buttons
and let my body spiral into a spray of red roses.
How it was
just you and me,
your green plaid shirt,
our smiles; even now
the taste on our tongues.

Outside The Basilica

Children beg
on the streets of Rome.
Stealing is the art they learn

from their gypsy parents,
a way to survive the gold
glitter inside the Basilica.

They are the sacrifices
offered by their parents.
Their small brown bodies

taken from beds
to lie in the laps
of women with slick black hair

faceless behind newspapers
as their sons slice the traveler's bag,
pull out the day's indulgences.

My Father's Hands

There he is again, that same fat wren
hobbling around my backyard.
I thought his wing was broken.

I offered my crumbs but he flew away.
Here I am, captive on a bus full
of seniors heading for Atlantic City.

From my window I watch wrens fly
from tree to tree and think of my father
sitting on our porch swing without shoes,

string in hand ready to pull the upright shoe box
over an open mouth wren. *I just want
to see if I can capture it.*

My father worked in the steel mill.
I suppose he should have had
rough hands. He didn't.

I loved the gentle way his hands
held his harmonica captive.
The way his fingers

touched the instrument's edges
releasing
the melody of his breath.

Fallen

I will not visit my sister
in the hospital tomorrow.

And suddenly
the crucifix
hanging from
the gold chain
around my neck
falls
and lands
face down
on the floor
near my right foot.

I try
to remove
the gold chain
without Christ
hanging from it.

The clasp refuses to open
as if God is angry
that I will not look
at suffering's ugly face

as if God is saying
a gold chain without
Christ hanging from it
will strangle me anyway.

Sanctuary

The glitter of light
promises
a golden path
to holiness
but its glare
can blind us
to truth,

can lead
to a purple room
where a woman
with forlorn eyes
sits on a hard bench,
her left hand
to her ear
silencing yellow
sounds
of yesterday.

To enter
the sacred
she must climb
The ladder
of her own
cave.

Monstrance

Do you watch
from a window in the clouds
as I drown in rain

or are you rain
nourishing me as I stand
raw under a naked tree?

I pray to a piece of bread
inside a clear window
surrounded by gold.

You are more than bread.
You are tree, leaf, man, woman,
sun, moon, wind and stone.

you are invisible
fire
lighting the dark.

Walking Down Las Cruces Road

(Taos, New Mexico 8/13/11)

It was the road I wanted to walk.
I heard music as an old
black Chevy thumped past me.

Two young men bounced in the front seat,
a cigarette hanging from the mustached
mouth of the driver, a Corona
spilling in his buddy's hand.

I followed the music
reverberating from a house behind
an abandoned yellow school bus.

Along the roadside:
old tires, a rusty hot water tank,
broken glass, smashed oil and beer cans
and bees hovering over
an uneven splintered fence.

Then I saw them:
a man singing in time
to a lively Spanish tune
blaring through an open window
as he tossed laundry to a woman
with long dark hair, hips swaying
with each piece of clothing
flung across a frayed clothesline.

Christmas in Verona

Only on cold nights when I am alone
in my four bedroom house, my husband snoring
through my dreams, my children away
tucked in their new lives
do I want to crawl between the cobwebs,
wrap myself in that small bedroom
on James Street and remember being
one of five children huddled
in the warmth of Grandma's
feather mattress flopped
against a cold hardwood floor.

Her black hightop shoe held
the window beside her brass bed
high enough to echo her dry cough
down through the cobblestone alley
where the pine tree waited
under a thick white blanket.

On the wooden chest
beside the statue of St. Joseph
the clock ticked toward
morning's promise:
Women rolling ravioli dough,
pouring cups of *Eight O'Clock* coffee,
men drinking shots of *Four Roses* whiskey
singing, "Buen Natale."

After Fifty Years of Marriage

I've decided my body is perfect
with breasts hanging like fallen melons
and skin spotted, but always soft.

My rounded stomach looks like a road map
with all its stretch marks and cracks.
It tells me only where I've been,
not where I should go.

I like the way
my husband becomes excited
when he touches my dimpled buttocks.

I don't like when he yells,
Turn off the light
while I'm trying to read.

He doesn't know
I turn all the lights on in our house
after he retires to
to his favorite chair,
raises his feet
on a wooden stool
and falls asleep.

I regret nothing in my life
except
I didn't stay in Paris
with that other man.

Ascension

I want to look in that room one more time
before my dark eyes shut their lids
and bury the old mahogany bed
draped in the desert linen
of your grandparents.
I want to watch our naked bodies
glisten in the vanity mirror
as your hands cup my breasts
unraveling my heart's smallest details
like a spool of colored thread
and your mouth covers my fevered
flesh like a soft poultice.
I want to hear you whisper
my name again and again.
This time I will erase time
flashing like flames.
This time the fire in my heart
will burn your tears to ashes
that ascend in clouds
where the air eats everything.

Baby Love
for Jolie

I was a first grader the year I waited on my porch step
for the tornado to pass. It was my seventh birthday,
the seventh time my mother recited the saga of my birth,
her labor from Holy Thursday until Easter Sunday.

Standing outside the hospital room on your birth day,
I cringed at each of your mother's birthing cries,
remembered the day I gave birth to her,
waited for her door to open to the wake of you.

I wanted your eyes blue and coupled to mine, forever.
But your eyes turned hazel,
your crawl became a walk,
and then you ran into my arms, a toothless first grader.

Malocchio
(evil eye)

When our daughter was born
Zia Lucia said, *Don't say she's beautiful.*
Don't even think it without saying,
God bless her. And don't forget
to pin holy medals in her crib
to ward off the evil eye.

I did as she said, half-believing, remembering

Zia Janina sitting on a red chrome chair,
too small for her hanging flesh,
as she made the sign of the cross
on our mother's aching forehead
then added a few drops of oil
to water in a white porcelain bowel
and began chanting prayers in Italian.

Viene qui she called to my sister and me
hiding behind her laced kitchen curtains.
Guardare. Mama got mal'occhio bad, real bad
as oil formed little golden rings in the water
then spread wide as our eyes.

Holy Thursday

I think of her as I crack eggs,
my floured hands sticking to shells,
the yeast swelling inside a cup of warm water.

It is Holy Thursday, 1950.
Grandma sucks a lemon drop as we climb
the steep hill to Saint Joseph's Church.
If she is tired, she never complains.
The priest blesses and breaks the host.
Her small head bows inside her black *sciarpa*.
The hump on her back more obvious
as she leans forward on the kneeler.
Her rosary shakes in hands that earlier shook
around a floured rolling pin

while Cousin Mary and I knelt on wooden chairs,
cracked eggs inside the blue rim bowl, then turned
their shells down on the pasta dish to drain.
Nothing was wasted in Grandma's house.

She will brush the whites on the *Easter Pizza Piano,*
carve the sign of the cross in the mound of dough
ready for the oven,
"Nel nome del padre, figlio e spirito santo.
Gals, fate presto per andare a chiesa!"

Her broken English ascending
from the corners of my kitchen.

Three Billy Goats Gruff: Improvisation

In April at night
when the rest of us sleep
trees bloom little by little

quietly like my grandsons
who walk in woods with me
this rainy morning,

boots squishing under budding forsythia
little heads bobbing
under green and blue umbrellas.

Dragging ball, bat and glove
over shiny wet stones,
we come to a wooden bridge

make believe the crooked
tree stump with exposed roots
underneath is an ugly troll.

We are the three Billy Goats Gruff.
The little one crosses first
then his bigger brother

and then me.
I say I will kill
the mean old troll.

Too late,
he dead
the little one says

as his older brother
aims his weapon at the tree stump
and relieves himself.

Emmanuel

I saw You today
in the face of the old
woman picking up dead
leaves in her driveway.

It wasn't how I imagined
You'd look. Her eyes
were dull, maybe blue
or brown. I can't remember.

I do remember the sores
weeping below her lips,
around her ears and cheeks.
Even on her balding scalp.

She must have noticed me staring.
I had cancer. Lost my breast.
My husband is sick now.
Smoked too much.

My children don't care.
You know how it is.
Busy with their own lives.
I thought of us

how we go about our busy lives
vowing to clean up our clutter
another day, telling ourselves
there will be plenty of time.

The Voice

Habibi, habibi
Not what I expected.
More like a hushed wind
stirring in my soul.

My beloved. Come,
Listen
I am—
the mystery
scattered throughout my Universe.

It does not matter
what piece, what size, what color,
whether you fit
at the beginning, end or center.

Your purpose
is to find your place
among the others,
so that one day

all may join
to give my voice
a face.

Truth

In the car,
last night's supper sticks in her throat.
A steady burn persists in her stomach.

She adjusts the rear view mirror.
A sagging face glances back.
There are so many

cars behind,
an empty highway ahead.
She turns on the ignition

revs up the engine,
thinks blue, the color of blood
before it leaves the body.

Remaking Driftwood

In my next life
let me come back a box.

I will lie waiting under the Mediterranean.
A sudden wave will wash me ashore.

Some young boy who looks like our son
will find me and bring me home

to his shed where he will carefully
unwrap carving tools and begin to remake

me into a wooden box, small
but big enough to hold the colored

fragments of your body, copper
like your skin, brown like your eyes

pieces of scattered shells that refuse
to leave after a stormy life.

This time I promise to hold
you safe inside me,

to treasure the sanctity
of what remains.

Grandma You Have Followed Me to These Bean Fields in Cordova, New Mexico

Together we walk the years
down another dirt road in Verona, Pennsylvania
when the blue bandanna
lifts strands of silver from your parched face.
Your callused hands pick raspberries
creeping from wooden fences,
plop them gently into your folded apron.
Cousin Mary skips ahead bouncing pick and shovel.
I lag behind, spilling water from filled buckets.

For dust thou art…
and unto dust thou shall return.
(Genesis 3:15)

It lies there
wanting nothing.
Its own beginning.
Its own end.

Why do we
blow it from our beds
wipe it from our counters
chase it out of our homes
only to find it
on a favorite chair,
inside a shoe,
stuck to our necks?

A speck
of dust,
our connection
to each other
begins
and ends
within itself.

A speck
of dust,
reminds us
we shall return
and return
and return.

ACKNOWLEDGMENTS

Some of the poems in this book first appeared in the following publications, sometimes in different versions and/or different titles: *Earth Daughters* ("Roots"); *Edge* ("My Father's Hands"); *Encore* ("There is a Thief Who Robs from Us"); *Evening Street Review* ("Anxiety My Familiar"); *First Decade* ("Your Green Plaid Shirt"); *Flash!Point* ("Mrs. Angelo's Daughter"); *Hudson View* (I Can Only Imagine); *Loyalhanna Review* ("Beyond," "Dreamer," "Grandma, You Have Followed Me to Cordova, New Mexico"); *Main Street Rag* (Even at Five); *Pittsburgh City Paper* ("Julia," "My Green Velvet Purse"); *Pittsburgh Post Gazette* ("Canning Tomatoes," "I Want to Be One of Those Green Beans in the Photograph on the Fifth Floor of Shadyside Hospital," "October in Pittsburgh," "On the Eve of Christmas," " Mike the Bum"); *Pittsburgh and Tri-State Area Poets* ("When Love Speaks"); *Poetry Magazine* ("Returning," Chicken Soup," "Canning Tomatoes"); *Rune* ("Walking Down Las Cruces Road"); *Steam Ticket* ("Yellow"); *The Panhandler* ("Love Song"); *The Pennsylvania Review* ("Moon's Child"); *The Pittsburgh Quarterly* ("Chicken Soup," "Your Path"); *Time of Singing* ("Emmanuel," "Monstrance"); *Verve* ("Returning"); *Voices in Italian Americana* ("Christmas in Verona," Holy Thursday"); *Voices from the Attic* ("Split," "The Music Room at Niagara on The Lake," "Three Billy Goats Gruff: Improvisation," "What You Must Never Forget"); *Z Miscellaneous* ("Ascension," "Separate")

I am most grateful to Maggie Anderson, who has left an indelible effect on my writing. I am thankful to the late Patricia Dobler, the late Sue Saniel Elkind, Lynn Emanuel and Dr. Ellie Wymard for their teaching guidance. Many thanks to Dr. Samuel Hazo for his encouragement and continued support. A special thanks to Jan Beatty, my longtime friend and mentor whose manuscript class made all the difference in the revisions to *Split*. I appreciate the many helpful suggestions from the members of the following poetry groups: the late Anita Byerly's Little Workshop, Liane Norman and The Informal Madwomen Workshop and Rosaly Roffman and the Squirrel Hill Poetry Workshop. Thanks to Jamie Benjamin for the cover design and drawing of *Split*, to Pamela O'Brien for reviewing and endorsing Split, to my confidant, Kathy Kirby Jones for her enduring friendship and to Antonio Morrone for his English to Italian translations. An extra special thanks to my husband of fifty-two years, Michie Samraney who has stood by me through all the phases of my life and to our extraordinary family: our daughter and my photographer, Marlo, our son-in-law Bob, our grandchildren Jolie, Nina, Zachary and Justin Oswald, and our son Danny and daughter-in-law Melissa Samraney for their unconditional love and support.

Joanne Matone Samraney, a retired Human Resources Director, lives in Pittsburgh, Pennsylvania with her husband of over fifty years, their two children and spouses and four grandchildren. She graduated magna cum laude from Carlow University in 1998 when her first grandchild was born. She is the recipient of the 2001 Acorn-Rukeyser Chapbook Award for her first chapbook, *Grounded Angels* published by Mekler & Deahl. Her second chapbook, *Remaking Driftwood* was published in 2010 by Finishing Line Press. She has also co-authored *Breaking Bread with the Boscos,* a collection of family memoirs and recipes published by Morris Press in 2001. Her work has appeared in numerous literary magazines and anthologies such as *Earth's Daughters, Voices in Italian Americana, A Hudson's View, Evening Street Review, Edge, Time of Singing, Voices from the Attic, Along These Rivers, The Potter's Wheel* and *Pittsburgh Post Gazette's Verse Envisioned.* She was a finalist in both the *Panhandler* and *Perivale* poetry chapbook contests for her manuscript, *Believe the Leaves.* She received an honorable mention for the Betty Gabelhart Poetry Prize Contest and was first runner up in Volume V, of the Loyalhanna Review. She has read her work on National Public Radio's Prosody, WYEP, was a member of The International Poetry Forum's Board of Associates and was part of a performance poetry group called, *Tea Time Ladies.*

www.ingramcontent.com/pod-product-compliance
Lightning Source LLC
Chambersburg PA
CBHW031224090426
42740CB00007B/704